# I spy under the sea...

## EDWARD GIBBS

B‖F‖&‖F

BRUBAKER, FORD & FRIENDS

AN IMPRINT OF THE TEMPLAR COMPANY LIMITED

D1438210

I spy with my little eye...

something with
a **stripy body**.

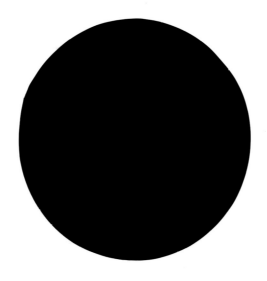

I have
a funny
name.

There are **seven** clownfish!
Can you count them?

7

I spy with my little eye…

something with
a **curly tail**.

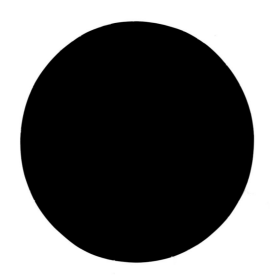

I am named
after an animal
you can ride.

There are **six** sea horses! Can you count them?

6

I spy with my little eye...

something with
**big claws**.

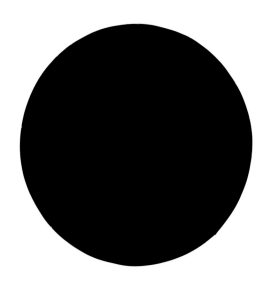

I walk
sideways on
the beach.

**5**

There are **five** crabs!
Can you count them?

I spy with my little eye...

something with
a **sharp nose**.

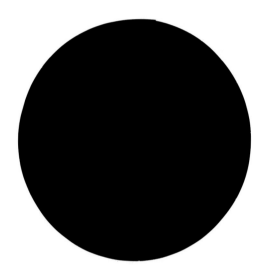

I am one of
the fastest fish
in the ocean.

There are **four** swordfish!
Can you count them?

4

I spy with my little eye...

something with
**lots of arms**.

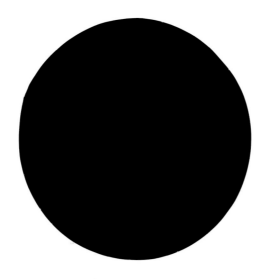

My arms
are called
tentacles.

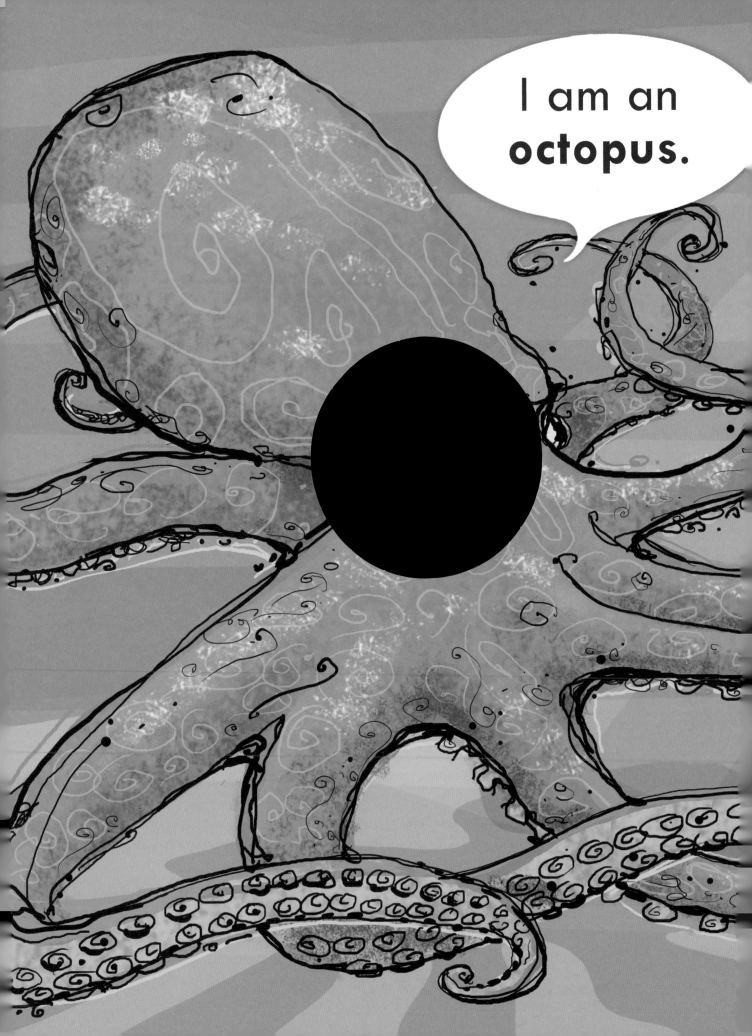

There are **three** octopuses!
Can you count them?

3

I spy with my little eye…

something with
**little flippers**.

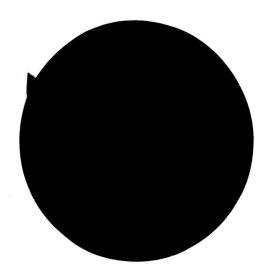

I love to
jump and play
in the water.

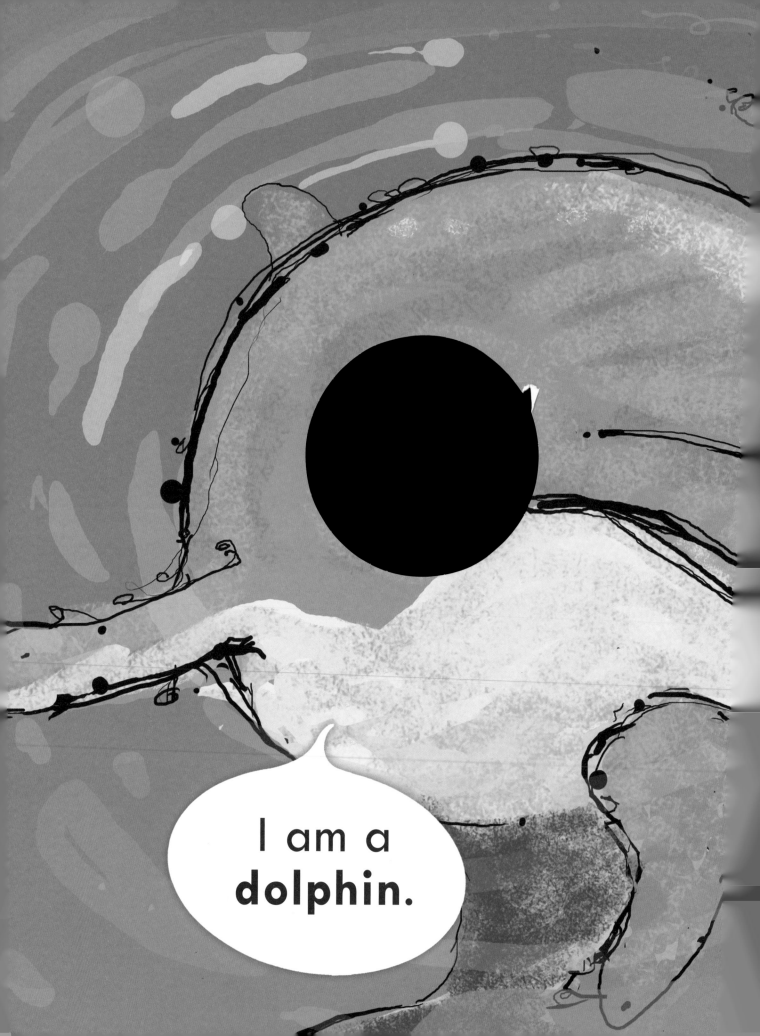

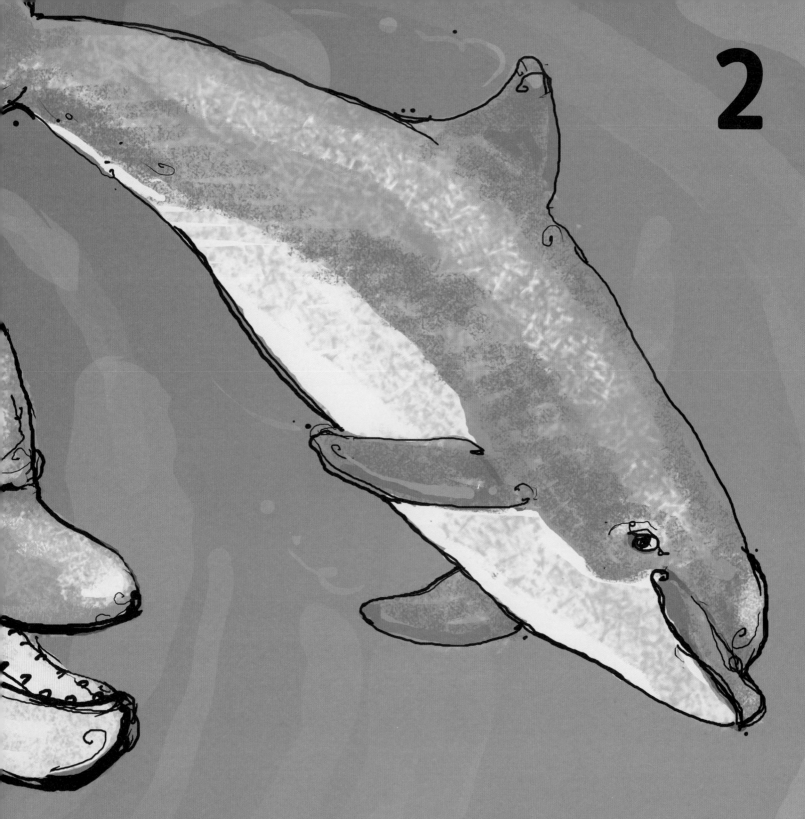

**2**

There are **two** dolphins!
Can you count them?

I spy with my little eye...

something with
a **big fin**.

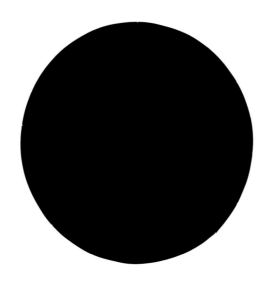

I am one of
the scariest creatures
in the sea.

What can **you** spy with **your** little eye?

# To Maria, with love

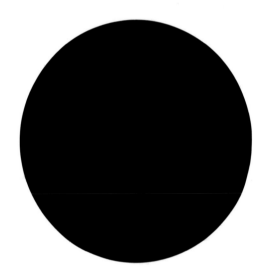

A BRUBAKER, FORD & FRIENDS BOOK,
an imprint of The Templar Company Limited

First published in the UK in hardback in 2011 by Templar Publishing
This softback edition published in 2012 by Templar Publishing,
The Granary, North Street, Dorking, Surrey, RH4 1DN, UK
www.templarco.co.uk

Copyright © 2011 by Edward Gibbs

First softback edition

ISBN 978-1-84877-731-6

Printed in China